Worthy

10 Days of Remembering
Who God Says You Are

A Detangled & Free Devotional by Kelsee Keitel

To every girl who has wondered if she really matters:
You matter. This book is dedicated to you.

TABLE OF CONTENTS

INTRODUCTION

WHY WE REMEMBER

In a performance-based world, run by resumes and sustaining an attractive social media persona, it's easy for our identity to become foggy. In our quest for becoming a good mom, a fun friend, a loving wife, a winning athlete, or a successful student, we let our work define who we are.

This doesn't feel like a problem when we are successful in these roles... However, when the good mom gets her teen's door slammed in her face with an "I hate you," or when the loving wife becomes the *nagging* wife...these roles are no longer as fulfilling as we had initially thought. When the star athlete is benched for a hip injury, or when the solid student is barely passing, the seeds to an identity crisis are planted.

We begin to grasp at *anything* that will give us a positive sense of identity. The immediacy of this search is then heightened when we look around and feel as though every other woman has got her act together. When no one else seems to be having this crisis, insecurity strikes. We compare ourselves to others, hoping to find someone a little less put-together than us - someone in the room who is just a bit more broken so that we can feel at least somewhat solid.

As long as I'm not the worst in the room...

We've forgotten who we are, yet our identity remains the same; if we would only look in the right place to find it. The Lord has named us and describes us in His Word. Because He is an all-knowing, never-failing God, what He says goes. And because He is never changing, what He says *stays*, regardless of our performance on the earth.

I have personally learned that if I don't know who I am in Christ, I fall into a cycle of striving – striving for love, approval, affirmation, perfection... you name it! Yet when I know who I am in Christ, and stand firm in this identity, I am able to rest.

So much of sin, heartache, and struggle come from approaching this world with a blank name-tag, offering a marker to *anyone* who will pen us an identity - a boyfriend, a teacher, a group of friends. We place our identity in the hands of others at the expense of our own intrinsic value. But this is not the answer to our identity crisis.

Someone might tell us we are chosen, worthy of love, and accepted... but those words only go so deep. Remembering stories about God's character, and how we've experienced Him personally will provide the reinforcement we need in order to truly believe in who God says we are.

Instead of creating an identity for ourselves or allowing someone else to choose an identity for us, we need to REMEMBER the identity that God has given us in Christ. Like an echo bouncing off the walls of a cave, when we remember who God is and what He has done, that truth will ricochet off the walls of our hearts and reflect who we are in Him.

It takes intentionality to embrace the identity God has for us. In this fast-paced world, we don't spend very much time remembering, but in biblical times, remembering was often a practical way to worship God and re-align the heart.

For example, after God miraculously made the Jordan River shallow enough for the Israelites to cross and escape from their enemies, Joshua led his people in an act of *remembrance*. He did this by raising up an Ebenezer stone that would commemorate what God had done *(Joshua 3)*. This was intended to help them remember God's faithfulness, and in turn, help them to trust God in the future.

When Jesus had His last supper with the disciples, He gave them bread and wine and told them to take these elements in *remembrance* of Him *(Luke 22:19-20)*. These items represented His soon-to-be beaten body and spilled blood. They didn't know it then, but Jesus was preparing His followers for a time when their hearts would need to be *consistently* reminded of who God is and what He had done in their lives, because He would no longer be present with them in the flesh.

I believe this act of remembrance was one of God's strategies for sustaining us through this world until we meet Him again. Like the disciples, we are commanded by God to actively and intentionally remember Him, what He has done, and what He taught. In order to claim our true identity, we must remember our Creator.

HOW TO REMEMBER

So maybe you're on board and ready to remember who God is...but you're not sure how to start. For me, remembering the Lord has three parts to it.

First, I open my Bible.

The Bible is compiled of direct accounts of what Jesus did, history of Christians and the Church, poetry, symbolic stories, and letters. Every passage in the Bible has something to reveal to us about God's character. In fact, God even goes so far as to calling Himself "The Word" *(John 1:1)*. When I remember His Word, and what it says, and what God did in biblical history, I am arming myself with truth to help me face the lies I encounter in this world - including lies about my identity.

Second, I remember what God has done in the lives of people I know.

I take note of how I've watched the Lord provide for my suffering friend, heal a sick family member, and answer bold prayers of the local church. In doing so, I notice how God's character is consistent from biblical times to present day.

Third, I remember what He has done in my personal life.

The world may chalk up certain events in my life as coincidence, luck, or happenstance. However, little moments that once seemed insignificant have God's handprints all over them when I look back in retrospect with a lens of remembrance.

Here is a real life example of what this remembrance looks like in action:

I was placed on a waiting list for a couple months before being allowed to start college. Some may say this was bad luck, but when I look back, I see that this was God's way of humbling me and showing me that His grace was the *only* reason I was able to get into my school of choice. My college years were very difficult at times, but through it all I was able to *remember* that God graciously brought me *to* school, so I could trust He would bring me *through* school. And He did! Now, whenever life seems to be taking a turn down an unexpected path, I remember my college journey, and that while God may be mysterious, He is always good.

Remembering what He has done in my own life helps me believe that He is a personal and relational God, and that He is just as active in my own life as He was in the lives of people I read about in the Bible.

This ten-day devotional was written with these three parts in mind. Each day is packed with biblical accounts, some of my personal experiences, a prayer, and reflective questions meant to help you remember what the Lord has done in your life, in order to claim the identity He has for you.

Each day of the devotional is spilt into two parts:
Part One: You Are
Part Two: Remember

Part One introduces that day's topic of who God says you are. I hope this section feels as if two old friends are grabbing some donuts on a Saturday morning, just encouraging one another through life.

Part Two will be more interactive on your part, as we dive deeper into specific scripture. This section will focus on an aspect of God's character and what He has done in your personal life - reinforcing the identity you've been reading about.

A FINAL ENCOURAGEMENT

Humans are naturally forgetful. We process so much information in a day that our brains have to do *something* with the information that isn't most important. Consequently, it may take some time for you to actually remember the experiences this devotional will ask you to recount. These questions are intended to make you slow down, think deeply, and reflect in a way that you may not be accustomed to in our fast-paced world.

As you work through this book, you may be tempted to believe a few statements like: *God isn't that active in my life. I've only been a Christian for a few years; He hasn't done that much yet. My testimony isn't that exciting.*

I challenge you over these next ten days to be open-minded. Pray to the Lord and ask Him to reveal Himself to you. Ask Him to help you remember. He will not ignore this kind of request because He loves to show Himself to His children. Jesus tells us to "ask and it will be given to you; seek and you will find; knock and the door will be opened to you. For everyone who asks receives; he who seeks finds; and to him who knocks, the door will be opened" (Luke 11:9-10).

Finally...there are no rules.

You'll notice I have provided spaces for you write in.
I know what it's like to be paralyzed by the fear of ruining a workbook or messing it up. But this devotional is for YOU. So write your thoughts...Scratch them out...Leave it blank and use your favorite journal...Read it ten days in a row...Read it once a week... Do whatever works best for you. This book is meant to assist you in growing closer to the Lord in whatever way works for you, so grab your favorite warm beverage and cozy on up for a sweet time of remembrance. I'll be right there with you, herbal tea with extra honey in hand.

With Love & Freedom,
Kelsee

YOU ARE CHOSEN

"My calendar is my LIFE!" I stated, as I held up my polkadot agenda book, quickly thumbing through it. After a few more minutes of rambling on about my organizational skills, and why I would make a great vice president of my high school club, I sat down. I had waited three years for this moment and I felt pretty good about what I had presented.

After a moment of applause, my single opponent stood to begin her speech.

"Some people say their calendar is their life...but I have TWO calendars that are my life."

The air in the room suddenly grew very dense. A swarm of eyes, accompanied by whispers fluttered from one another, to me, and then back to my running mate.

This still goes down as one of the most awkward and uncomfortable moments I've ever endured. At the time, I took my peer's statement as a personal attack (I was a seventeen-year-old girl, brought up on *Mean Girls* and *Lizzie McGuire*, after all.). Looking back in retrospect, I now see the deeper issue at hand...My competitor desperately wanted to be chosen for the role, and she was willing to go great lengths in order to make that happen.

She wasn't the only one though. I wanted to be chosen too. We *all* long to be chosen in one way or another.

Chosen by...the boss...the grad program...the parents...the friends...the guy...the sorority house...

When we find ourselves on the sideline, watching another girl being picked for our dream program, or another woman bursting with joy as the man of her dreams lowers to one knee...we feel very...*un*-chosen. Left out in the dust. Rejected. Knowing this, we're often desperate to avoid rejection - doing whatever it takes to be chosen and accepted.

The truth is, we don't need to act with such desperation because we each *have* been chosen - intentionally pursued by a God who stops at nothing until He has our heart and has it in full.

God's intentionality is written all over the story of how I first became a Christian. In the summer of 2008, I was *the most* boy-crazy girl. I was giggly and flirtatious, and always had my eye on someone. I had a deep desire to be known, loved, and chosen. Later that school year, my first real boyfriend invited me to church and would eventually introduce me to Jesus.

This relationship was quite strategic on God's part. God wanted my heart, and He knew how deeply I desired to be loved and cared for. He also knew that if any flashing, neon sign would catch my attention at that time in my life, it would be in the form of a boy. So He lovingly used what He *knew* would catch my attention.

God knows the deepest corners of your heart. He knows the one thing that makes you tick, makes you stop in your tracks, and causes you to say, "I want in." Like anyone who wants something strong enough, He pursues us accordingly.

Although my romantic relationship faded after a few years, I was left with something so much better: a relationship with the God of the universe. He chose me, and His intentionality caused my heart to choose Him right back.

You may be rolling your eyes, thinking, *"That's* not the kind of chosen I want to be," or "Why does *she (the girl whose relationship you're jealous of)* get to be the special kind of chosen, and I get to be *this* kind of chosen?"

Coincidentally, we want to choose how we are chosen - we'd much rather be chosen by a guy outside our window, standing in a circle of candles, singing *Yellow* by *Coldplay*, acoustic guitar in hand, than by a God who claims to be our Father. Maybe in order to be chosen, we've got to lay down our own ideas of what that should look like and accept that we already *are* chosen. Maybe we're standing in our own way of this joyous relationship!

If I could revisit that high school classroom, standing face to face with my running mate, I would show her so much more compassion than I actually did. I would tell her that she's not alone, and that I, too, desperately long to be chosen. I would tell her that she doesn't have to work so hard to be accepted, because she already has been.

I may not be able to travel back in time, but I can tell you, dear friend, the same thing: You don't have to work for acceptance because God has already done the heavy lifting. He sent His son to die so that you would be blameless before God and *worthy* of His choosing. This was all a part of His grand, intentional plan to pursue your heart.

REMEMBER HIS PURSUIT

We can trust that God has chosen us, when we pay careful attention to the way He has intentionally pursued each of us as unique individuals.

> "…for you are a people holy to the Lord your God. Out of all the peoples on the face of the earth, the Lord has chosen you to be his treasured possession."
> Deuteronomy 14:2 (NIV)

As you think about the way God pursues His chosen people, consider the disciple Thomas. When Jesus appeared to the eleven other disciples after His resurrection, Thomas was skeptical.

> "Unless I see the nail marks in his hands and put my finger where the nails were, and put my hands into his side, I will not believe." John 20:25 (NIV)

This is how He earned his nickname, "Doubting Thomas." But Jesus had already chosen Thomas. He loved Thomas. He had a plan for Thomas's life. Jesus knew exactly what He needed to do in order to help Thomas believe. About a week later, the scriptures tell us, Jesus came to Thomas and said,

> "Put your finger here; see my hands. Reach out your hand and put it into my side. Stop doubting and believe."
> John 20: 27 (NIV)

Because God pursued Thomas where He was, with all of his doubt, Thomas believed! God cared so much for Thomas that He was willing to do exactly what he claimed would help him believe.

Imagine how Thomas must have felt in that moment - realizing not only that Jesus was alive, but that He *loved* Thomas despite his disbelief. Jesus won Thomas's heart in a way that only Jesus

Himself could. No one else could satisfy Thomas's doubt. Jesus gave him exactly what he needed.

This is the same kind of intentionality that God used to help *me* believe, and if you reflect deeply, I'm confident you'll find that Jesus has been just as intentional with *you*.

Each story of coming to Christ is different and unique.
Maybe He sought you through loving parents who raised you to know Him.
Maybe He used friends or a missionary to share His love with you.
Perhaps you witnessed a miracle that pointed to no other explanation.

How ever you came to know Christ and fall in love with Him - it was His divine choosing of you, and His intentionality that first drew you to Him.

How has God pursued a relationship with you?

What was special about His pursuit that caused your heart to change from disbelief to belief?

When you begin to doubt your value, and compare the way others seem to be loved, remember God's passionate pursuit of you, chosen one.

Prayer For The Day

Dear Lord,
Thank you for choosing me, even when the world rejects me. Help me to stop striving after the approval of others, and help me to recognize that being chosen by You is better. No other relationship can compare to Yours. Give me fond memories of Your pursuit, and never let me forget how intentional and passionate You are. Let these memories make my heart beat deeper in love with You.
Amen.

YOU ARE ENOUGH

I was a competitive dancer for about fifteen years. Around the time that I turned ten years old, I realized that winning wasn't as easy as it was when I was a cute five-year-old prancing around with puckered lips. There was now a higher expectation for skills and substance in my dancing. It was about this time that I noticed I wasn't as natural at dancing as many of my peers were. I was talented, but I had to work twice as hard as some of my classmates. Despite my best efforts, there were some tricks I just wasn't able to master. Consequently, my routines were judged as less impressive.

Maybe there are some tricks you can't seem to tackle. If you're anything like me, you look at other women with a hint of bitterness in your heart, wondering why you just can't be like her.

If only I had what she has... then I'd be content.

There's no denying we live in a competitive world; one in which we feel the constant pressure to compensate for where we are lacking. There are eyebrow crayons to help us create a symmetrical face, countless "quick" weight loss products, and tanning bed businesses on every corner - and these examples only skim the surface of our *physical* appearance. We're tempted daily to take our worth into our own hands and do everything in our power to be *enough*.

This is no new problem. We see this two thousand years ago in biblical times when Jesus visits with Mary & Martha at their home. Mary sat at Jesus's feet and enjoyed just being in His presence. Her sister Martha, on the other hand, was running around the house working and cleaning in order to impress their guest. Jesus told Martha that she had her priorities all wrong and that *"Mary has chosen what is better"* by being still with Him *(Luke 10:38-42).*

I can identify so much with Martha - trying to catch all my bearings to get my life together, doing all that I can to impress Jesus the same way I try to impress those around me. In reality, Jesus makes it clear that resting and basking in His presence is the best choice we can make.

God isn't like the rest of the judges we're used to impressing. He doesn't ask for special tricks or perfect first impressions. He can't be persuaded. He doesn't take bribes. He sees us, He knows us, and He says, "Just be with me. You are enough for me."

REMEMBER HIS GRACE

We are a "fix it" people – prone to search for the quickest solution to any deficits we see, including within ourselves. Yet God calls us to embrace stillness in His presence. We aren't enough on our own. We have been made enough however, by God's grace, through Jesus. If only we would pause long enough to accept this grace.

> "Be still, and know that I am God..."
> Psalm 46:10 (NIV)

In what ways do you find yourself trying to compensate for the areas you feel inadequate, like Martha?

Read these words, of the apostle Paul:

> "For I am convinced that neither death nor life, neither angels nor demons, neither the present nor the future, nor any powers, neither height nor depth, nor anything else in all creation, will be able to separate us from the love of God that is in Christ Jesus our Lord." Romans 8:38-39 (NIV)

Highlight the things in the passage above that cannot separate us from Christ.

Nothing can separate you from God's love, including your greatest success and your worst shortcomings. Jesus did all the compensation for us, and when He was done, hanging on the cross... what did He say?

Answer: *It is* _____. *(John 19:30)*

That means there is no work on your part to be done in saving yourself. It wasn't always like this though...

Before Jesus died, if a person did something wrong or fell short, she would have been required to make a blood sacrifice, by killing a special animal. In order to be in good standing with God, a sacrifice had to be made. Can you imagine how stressful that would be? Always trying to be as good as you possibly could, or else you'd be required to make a sacrifice?

Over time, this world became so broken that no man-made sacrifice would be sufficient. So God provided a perfect, all sufficient sacrifice for us: Jesus.

Once Jesus came to this earth and died, He became the ultimate sacrifice to cover all of the sins and shortcomings of the world, including yours and mine. We did not deserve or earn Christ's sacrifice on our behalf, yet God still gave it to us. This is grace.

> "For it is by grace you have been saved, through faith – and this is not from yourselves, it is the gift of God – not by works, so that no one can boast." Ephesians 2:8-9 (NIV)

Take a pause, and receive God's grace today. You don't need to measure up to anyone, and you don't need to compensate for your areas of weakness. You can view these as areas of growth now. Because of God's grace, you are enough.

Prayer For The Day

Dear Lord,
Even though You paid the final sacrifice, I still find myself striving to earn Your love. Remind me that I am enough the way I am, not because of my goodness, but because of Jesus' goodness that now covers me. Help me to remember Your grace when I believe the lie that I am not worthy enough to approach You.
Love, Your Daughter

YOU ARE FULL OF POTENTIAL

I am a proud member of the *Hot Pocket* generation. There has never been a time in my life when it wasn't possible to heat up a meal in less than three minutes. I can send my friend in China a message and hear back from her in an instant. I can skip the line at *Panera Bread*, grabbing my *Fuji Apple Chicken Salad* (extra dressing and hold the blue cheese, please), running in and out without speaking to a soul.

While instant gratification can be...well...gratifying, the fast-paced culture I've grown up in has a downside: I've come to expect instant results in every other area of my life. This impatience is especially evident in areas where I'm looking for growth and progress. When I'm not where I want to be yet, I become discouraged.

Maybe you can relate...
You're still trying to figure out what career path to take, while your best friend has known she would be a doctor since she received her first play stethoscope at her fourth grade birthday party. You can barely make it through a 5K, unlike your sorority sister, who just completed her first mini marathon. You feel awkward during prayer, while your roommate makes talking to God look so easy...

All this can make you feel behind, and a little less valuable than your friend who seems to be cruising right along. But I want to tell you a secret:

Just because you're not where you want to be, doesn't mean you're useless right now. And it doesn't mean you're doomed. It means you're not done yet. You're not done growing. Not done learning. Not done discovering your full potential.

It's okay to hope for growth and to strive to be better or different. And it's possible to do so while simultaneously being content with how things are in the present.

A few years ago, following some triggering events, I developed an anxiety disorder called Obsessive-Compulsive Disorder. OCD seemed to rule my life and made a few of my college years extremely difficult. However, after counseling and other modes of treatment, the Lord has given me a great deal of healing.

My healing wasn't a quick fix, though. You see, in the pit of my struggle I was *convinced* I'd be an anxious, obsessive, compulsive ball of stress for the rest of my life. Each day that OCD seemed to win, felt like one scoop deeper into the hole I was trapped in. I felt stuck. But God knew better. He knew I'd break free. He knew this particular struggle was going to grow me and glorify Him in the future. God saw my potential when I couldn't see it myself - the potential I had in Him.

I still have other struggles, but I've seen victory in this one. And you'll see victory in yours.

One of my favorite burger joints from my little college town, *Bub's Burgers & Ice Cream*, in Bloomington, Indiana has this encouragement printed at the bottom of their menu: "If we're busy, sit back and relax! Bub's will not compromise quality for speed!"

Read that again: "Bubs will not compromise quality for speed."

I'm taking a page out of Bub's book - er, menu. Here's my personal revision:

Kelsee _will not compromise quality for speed. While she could be rushing things along, wishing she were a few steps forward, she's choosing to rest and trust in the Lord's provision instead. She is confident in His timing and believes that He has good things planned out for her. She is willing to find long-lasting joy in the waiting rather than immediate, yet fleeting pleasure in speed. She's in this for long haul, with her trusty Savior at her side._

God has got good plans in store for us _(Jeremiah 29:11)_ because He cares for us _(1 Peter 5:7)._ We only need to be patient along the way.

It's easy to compare your progress to that of another girl...
She overcomes adversity so much quicker than I do.
She makes progress faster than me.
She bounces back so quickly.

Like a hike in the woods, we might take different trails and methods to get there. We all move at different speeds. The only way to lose is to stop moving. So don't let someone else's victory kick you to the bench. She's not your competitor, and her speed doesn't dictate yours. You've got potential. There's only a matter of time, before you see it revealed.

REMEMBER YOUR VICTORIES

One way to feel encouraged during a challenging time is to remember the way God has given us victory over past challenges.

"But thanks be to God! He gives us the victory through our Lord Jesus Christ." 1 Corinthians 15:57 (NIV)

Write about a struggle that you've had in the past (big or small, long-term or short-term) that you no longer face.

Did you ever feel like you would be stuck in that hard place forever?

How, by God's power and grace, did you overcome that adversity?

Praise God! You've seen the very unweaving of your potential. Let that victory be an encouragement when you face the next adversity.

"I have told you these things, so that in me you may have peace. In this world you will have trouble. But take heart! I have overcome the world." John 16:33 (NIV)

Not only does Jesus overcome the struggles of this world, but He gives us the ability to be thankful throughout our troubles.

"We can rejoice, too, when we run into problems and trials, for we know that they help us develop endurance. And endurance develops strength of character, and character strengthens our confident hope of salvation." Romans 5:3-4 (NLT)

According to Romans 5:3-4, problems and trials allow us to <u>develop</u>. What 3 characteristic traits does the writer tell us we have the potential to develop through difficulties?

What character traits have you developed through the struggles you have faced?

Read this excerpt from one of Paul's letters, Philippians 1:3-6

> I thank my God every time I remember you. In all my prayers for all of you, I always pray with joy because of your partnership in the gospel from the first day until now, being confident of this, **that he who began a good work in you will carry it on to completion until the day of Christ Jesus.** Philippians 1:3-6 (NIV, Emphasis Added)

Paul and Timothy are full of joy for the way they have seen the people of Philippi grow since they first started following God. They have full confidence that God, who created the first ounce of goodness in these people, will continue allowing them to grow, and become more like Jesus until He returns again.

This is good news for us! As long as we follow Jesus with our whole hearts and devote our lives to Him, we will be made more and more like Him until He returns and completes the work in us!

This is our greatest potential: becoming more like Christ.

Are you struggling to see the light at the end of a certain hardship right now? Explain.

How can remembering your past victories and character development give you strength in this particular trial?

In your moments of discouragement: Keep heart, reflect on your past victories, and remember that they are evidence of your potential in Jesus Christ.

_____ (your name) *will not compromise quality for speed. While she could be rushing things along, while wishing she was a few steps forward, she's choosing to rest and trust in the Lord's provision instead. She is confident in His timing and believes that He has good plans for her, and she is willing to find long-lasting joy in the waiting rather than immediate, yet fleeting, pleasure in speed. She's in this for long haul, with her trusty Savior at her side.*

Prayer For The Day

Heavenly Father,
Help me to remember my victories, and the ways You have
delivered me from trouble. I want to be strengthened and
encouraged by these moments. Help me to not fear trouble, but
welcome it, knowing it brings a new opportunity to draw nearer
to You. Give me a desire to become more like Jesus, even if that
means facing adversity. Help me to grow in endurance, character,
and hope, so that I can reach my fullest potential: becoming more
like Christ.
Your Daughter

YOU ARE WONDERFULLY DESIGNED

When I was growing up, my family referred to me as "sentimental" because I would cry very easily. This is still true of me today. It is not uncommon for me to get the waterworks running while watching a movie (which was supposed to be a comedy) or theatrical performance, receiving a kind note, or hearing a beautiful song. I feel things very deeply and my heart is touched easily.

There have been times in my life, particularly painful times, when I wished I wasn't like this though. Not only do I cry happy tears and sad tears; I cry tears of embarrassment, anger, and frustration. I remember being called out by a professor in college for answering a question incorrectly and it took everything within me to hold back the tears. I didn't *want* to cry; this was just my natural wiring. In this moment...red-faced, heart beating, surrounded by peers who probably wouldn't have cried if they were in my shoes...I resented my sensitivity. I wished I didn't care so much. I wished I could be more calloused.

Over time, I've realized that my sensitivity is not a character flaw, but a character strength. I've learned that God created me in my mother's womb with a tender heart, acute emotions, and a level of sympathy that many are unable to channel. Through time and experience, I've come to embrace that He wired me this way for His glory. I've been able to serve the Lord, with this central part of my personality, in a unique way that a less sensitive girl may not be able to.

I want you to know that the qualities deeply ingrained in you that you aren't thrilled about...those may actually be your greatest assets. Your weird laugh, introverted personality, funny birthmark, or unique passion that no one else shares...you don't have to treat them like shameful burdens worth trading. You can embrace them as gifts from God instead.

It's easy to look at others and wish we could be more like them. But you don't need to be more like *her*. You need to be more like *Jesus*. You were made in His image, after all *(Genesis 1:27)*.

God has a plan for *her,* and He has a plan for *you*. But it doesn't work very well if you're both the same person. Something is missing and that something is YOU. You were created in the depths of a woman's womb to give glory to God with your whole being. Not just your favorite parts of you, but *God's favorite parts of you.*

REMEMBER GOD'S INERRANCY

In this section, we will explore God's perfect creativity, and the way He uniquely, and intentionally designed you.

> "For you created my inmost being; you knit me together in my mother's womb. I praise you because I am fearfully and wonderfully made; your works are wonderful, I know that full well."
> Psalm 139:13-14 (NIV)

On the lines to the left, list 3 qualities you like about yourself. On the lines to the right, explain how you might give God glory with those qualities.

_____   _____

_____   _____

_____   _____

Now, list 3 of your qualities that you aren't particularly fond of and how you might give God glory with *those* qualities.

_____   _____

_____   _____

_____   _____

It may have been difficult to find ways to glorify God with the parts you don't like about yourself, because oftentimes we are distracted by how we can fix them in order to give *ourselves* glory. God is so glorious on His own, that it should not be too difficult for us to find ways to give Him glory. It all starts with having our focus on *His* glory, not our own.

Let's start now, by shifting our focus to God's creative abilities.

> "In his hand are the depths of the earth, and the mountain peaks belong to him. The sea is his, for he made it, and his hands formed the dry land." Psalm 95:4-5 (NIV)

> "The heavens declare the glory of God; the skies proclaim the work of his hands." Psalm 19:1 (NIV)

Think of the most beautiful landscape you've ever seen. God created that – every single detail. Psalm 8 tells us that God placed each star in the sky exactly where He wanted it.

Write out Psalm 18:30 below.

What does this imply about how you were designed?

What are 3 ways that you can show God you are thankful for the way He made you?

When you scroll through social media this week and wish you could be more like *Jordan*, smarter like *Josie*, as pretty as *Abby*, funny like *Emma*, and creative as *Nicole*...remember the words of Psalm 139:14. You are wonderfully designed by an inerrant God.

Prayer For The Day

Dear God,
I worship You now because You have made so much beauty, and you've made it without error. You are a perfect, intentional, and strategic creator. You are lovingly making me who I'm meant to be, like a potter gently shaping a ball of clay. Help me to embrace my personality, my appearance, my mind, and my heart out of worship for You. Allow me to lead other women in realizing how special and valuable each of them is, simply because of how creative You are. You defined beauty and then created beauty. You know beauty better than anyone. Give me confidence in your design, so that when the media sways my heart to disbelief, I can stand firm in the hands of my Perfect Creator.
Love, Your creation

YOU ARE STRONG

Have you ever had way too much on your plate? Your calendar is all filled in, so you spend a day trying to decide what to cut out, only to discover that every item is a priority. There's no escaping the deadlines, so you do what you can to survive.

When our hands are made too full, or a circumstance seems impossible to face, it's easy to feel like a tiny ant approaching an entire granny smith apple: helpless and overwhelmed.

We understand that God is big and powerful, but we're not quite convinced that we have any power ourselves. The temptations seem too strong. The circumstances are too hard. The weight of our responsibilities is too heavy.

We may even find ourselves saying, "God, how am I supposed to conquer this? I'm only human!"

Our real issue isn't all that we're facing; it's what we're *forgetting*: The Holy Spirit. We remember God the Father and Jesus the Son, but we often dismiss the third person of the Trinity.

Scripture tells us that when we believe in Jesus, His Holy Spirit enters inside of us *(Ephesians 1:13)*. The Holy Spirit then becomes our guide, helping us live a life that glorifies the Lord and makes us become more alive and more like Him, like we studied on *Day 4.*

Just how powerful is this Holy Spirit? This is the same spirit that raised Jesus from the grave. If you are a follower of Christ, this resurrecting spirit is inside of you! I don't know about you...but I can't think of any other spirit that is as powerful as one that can raise a dead man back to life.

> "And if the Spirit of him who raised Jesus from the dead is living in you, he who raised Christ from the dead will also give life to your mortal bodies because of his Spirit who lives in you." Romans 8:11 (NIV)

Perhaps the reason we find ourselves feeling so weak, is because we're sprinting through this life relying on our own strength, rather than the power of God inside of us. The Holy Spirit gives us the ability to change our "I can't," into "I can't on my own...but I *can* because He lives in me!"

REMEMBER HIS POWER

When Jesus sent His twelve disciples out into ministry, He commanded them to heal the sick and tell everyone about the kingdom of God *(Luke 10:9)*. Talk about an overwhelmingly large task!

But the book of Acts tells us that they did as they were commanded, even after Jesus was gone from the Earth.

> "The apostles performed many signs and wonders among the people...Crowds gathered also from the towns around Jerusalem, bringing their sick and those tormented by impure spirits, and all of them were healed." Acts 5:12 & 16 (NIV)

Did they heal people by their own human power? No.

Where did that power come from?

> "And I will ask the Father, and he will give you
> another advocate to help you and be with you forever
> – the Spirit of truth. The world cannot accept him,
> because it neither sees him or knows him. But you
> know him, for he lives with you and will be in you."
> John 14:16-17 (NIV)

The Holy Spirit performs miracles through average human beings everyday. One of the most commonly recognized miracles are the kind that happen in hospitals, when a doctor reports a healing that occurred with no other explanation than "someone was watching over you." But the Holy Spirit does much more than just medical miracles. He gives courage, strength, confidence, and resilience to those who otherwise may not have it *(Isaiah 40:29-31)*.

When have you witnessed God's power?

What does it mean to you to have that exact same power alive inside of you?

How can you be more aware of this power in your everyday life, for God's glory?

When you feel like a tiny ant, remember the resurrecting, wind-changing, wave-calming, cancer-curing power that lives inside you. Because He lives, you are strong in His power.

Prayer For The Day

Almighty Lord,
Thank you for allowing the powerful Holy Spirit to dwell inside of me. I want to be more aware of Him, not leaving Him out of my everyday life. Help me to recognize His resurrecting power that is flowing through my veins. Remind me to rely on You when I am weak and when I am confident. Help me to boast in you only, Lord. I'm expecting you to give me the strength to carry on, and thrive through my present struggles.
Love, Your Daughter

YOU ARE IMPORTANT

What is your initial response to hearing the words *group project?* If you're anything like me, there's an automatic groan, followed by an anxious bellyache. Those two words have been terrorizing students for years, as a crucial standard in education. Each group is different, yet there always seems to be that one person who just skims by, never really contributing anything. There's the "extreme Type-A personality" member who insists on doing most of the heavy labor. And then there's the in-between student, not really sure how much to participate; not wanting to do a lot, but not wanting to get docked points either.

Maybe you don't feel needed in God's plan. You don't feel helpful, because you don't know that much about the Bible. You still get nervous praying around others. You don't feel worthy of being a part of the team. You're too sinful, too hypocritical, too messy, too under qualified to be a contributing member of the group. My friend, that is just not true!

You've been invited into the greatest, longest-standing, most important group project in all of history, and you weren't invited because of what you have to offer; you were enlisted because of what God has to offer *through* you! We need all hands on deck for the good news of the gospel to reach *all* the ends of the earth. You are needed in this plan!

Your old group project dynamics in which you could add a few slides to the *PowerPoint* presentation, and tag on a few research articles that you didn't actually read (I may or may not be speaking from experience) are gone. We need everyone's best effort.

Today I am challenging you to stop comparing yourself to the girl who grew up in Sunday school, while you just became a Christian a few years ago. Your story is just as powerful as hers. You're work is just as important as hers. All you need is a heart that throbs for the Father and for His children to come home.

REMEMBER THE MISSION

This famous piece of scripture below is called the *Great Commission.* This is the mission Jesus gave His disciples, which still applies to us today.

> "Then the eleven disciples went to Galilee, to the mountain where Jesus had told them to go. When they saw him, they worshiped him; but some doubted. Then Jesus came to them and said, 'All authority in heaven and on earth has been given to me. Therefore go and make disciples of all nations, baptizing them in the name of the Father and of the Son and of the Holy Spirit, and teaching them to obey everything I have commanded you. And surely I am with you always, to the very end of the age.'"
> Matthew 28:16-20 (NIV)

Verse 17 says, "But some doubted."

Even though some of the disciples had their doubts, Jesus *still* sent them out on the mission. Sometimes we think that in order to be a part of God's mission, we have to know everything or be a "superstar Christian." That is a lie.
You don't have to be perfect to serve God. You just have to say, "Yes".

What are some insecurities or weaknesses you have that make you feel "not good enough" to serve God?

Despite your weakness, God has sent you out.

When I start to doubt my ability to contribute to God's mission, this quote from Bob Goff's book, *Love Does,* encourages my soul:

"I used to think you had to be special for God to use you, but now I know you simply need to say yes."

Reread Matthew 28:16-20.
In the Great Commission, there are 4 specific actions we are instructed to take. What do you think each of them mean?

Go:

Make Disciples:

Baptizing:

Teaching:

How can you live out this mission by using your unique gifts that we discussed in *Day 5* ?

Who has God placed in your life to share the good news of Christ with?

Remember, like we studied in *Day 5*, we can only fulfill this mission through God's Holy Spirit in us. It's not by our own power, but by His power inside of us. You have a choice as to whether you accept the mission or not; but one person cannot do it all - you are important in His mission.

Prayer For The Day

Dear Father,
I want to be an active member of Your team. I want share the
gospel to the lost and broken people of this world, just like
someone else shared it with me. Give me open ears and eyes to
notice moments when I can share Your good news. Help me be so
in-tune with The Spirit that I follow His lead in the mission field.
Remind me that I am on mission every day, everywhere. God,
when I feel unequipped, remind me that You equip those You call.
Take away any apathy from my heart and replace it with a
passion for Your mission.
Amen.

DAY 7

YOU ARE A WINNER

Have you ever witnessed a sore loser at a sporting event? I remember witnessing all sorts of tantrums and poor sportsmanship when my nephew was on a t-ball team. These young children were still learning what it meant to win and lose well, and, as a result, some kids would throw their bats, slam their helmets, and refuse to shake the winners' hands. And don't even get me started on the sore losing parental behavior...

Think about the worst loser you know, and the behaviors they exhibit.

Sore losers like to shame the winners into believing that they really didn't deserve the win, often by making accusations like, "you cheated!" or "those were terrible referees."

Christ won the battle of light and darkness, and we get to share in His victory *(1 Corinthians 15:57)*. Not only were you chosen for the team, you were chosen for the *winning* team.

But Satan, the devil, is THE sorest loser of them all. He refuses to believe that he has lost the fight of darkness and light, and will do everything he can to make you believe that you have lost too. The enemy is determined - I'll give him that.

He whispers this message to you each time you compare your "boring" life to the colorful social media account of a friend. Each time plans get cancelled and you find yourself alone on a Saturday night, he'll take that opportunity to foul you. When you feel frumpy and can't find a single item to wear to the party in your closet, he's there. We've got to immerse ourselves in the winning truth of the gospel if we're going to rise above Satan's lies.

Another characteristic of a sore loser is that they love a good rematch.

Even though he has lost the war, the enemy isn't backing down. He is still on the prowl, ready to steal, kill, and destroy *(John 10:10)*.

But when Jesus died that victorious death, He said three powerful words: It is finished *(John 19:30)*. This war is over.

Is the sore-losing enemy pushing you around? Do you feel like you're losing? Remember whose team you're on. The score is settled; you've already won. Proclaim that victory loud and proud and send the adversary back to where he came from.

REMEMBER THE SCORE

When we gaze out the office window, scroll through social media, or turn on the six o'clock news, it is easy for us to feel discouraged by the state of the world. There is a new tragedy each day. Senseless deaths are occurring. We still have no cure for cancer. Racial tension is still very alive. Human beings are being exploited, and money seems to be more important than innocent souls.

When it all adds up, we start to wonder if darkness has actually won. In order to cling on to hope, we must remember Christ's triumph over evil.

Remember Jesus's triumphant defeat of sin and darkness.

> "When you were dead in your sins and in the uncircumcision of your flesh, God made you alive with Christ. He forgave us all our sins, having canceled the charge of our legal indebtedness, which stood against us and condemned us; he has taken it away, nailing it to the cross. And having disarmed the powers and authorities, **he made a public spectacle of them, triumphing over them by the cross.**"
> Colossians 2:13-15 (NIV, Emphasis Added)

Team Satan: 0
Team Jesus: 1

Remember who you were before Jesus changed your life. What were you like before you knew Him, or before you truly started to follow Him?

How has knowing Jesus personally changed your life?

Team Satan: 0
Team Jesus: 2

The actual scoreboard of faith (if there was such a thing) would probably look more complicated than a simple 2-0. And don't get me wrong; Satan does win some battles from time to time. He is powerful. But we can be confident knowing that Christ is MORE powerful. He has won the war and will be victorious for all of eternity.

> "But thanks be to God! He gives us the victory
> through our Lord Jesus Christ!" 1 Corinthians 15:57
> (NIV)

Have you ever watched a game where someone accidently passed the ball to the opposing team, who then quickly scored a point? John Piper writes in his book *Spectacular Sins,*

"God did not just overcome evil at the cross. He made evil *serve* the overcoming of evil."

In other words, the devil's best play sent the ball straight into God's hands, where He scored the winning touchdown.

When the devil whispers those lies, calling you a loser, and when you start to think he might be right...remember whose team you're on. You are a winner according to the scoreboard of faith, and no one can take that victory away from you!

Prayer For The Day

Dear God,
Yours is the kingdom, the glory, and the power, forever. You have won the war of all wars. Thank you for sharing this victory with me. Help me proclaim this victory and stand firm in the truth of Romans 8, that there is no condemnation for those who love You. When I'm in the midst of a discouraging battle, help me remember that You have won the WAR, defeating death and darkness, once and for all.
Amen.

DAY 8

YOU ARE CARED FOR

When I was dating my husband, I wanted so badly for us to be engaged. I just wanted our love to be more...official...you know... shiny-ring-on-the-finger-official. I wanted to be able to plan my dream wedding, and to finally be able to say out loud what I knew in my heart - that we would be together forever. For real, forever.

Once we were finally engaged...you guessed it...I couldn't wait for us to be married. There were some weeks during the wedding planning process that I would throw my hands up in the air and say, "Let's just elope tomorrow instead!" My heart was done with that season of planning and waiting - I wanted to be Mrs. Keitel.

Now that we're married, I am pretty content with where our relationship is, but I still hope for new seasons at times. I'm looking forward to the day when we can move out of apartment living and into a house of our very own. I'm ready to graduate and start my counseling career. And although I haven't quite experienced this yet myself, I've heard that once the "baby fever" hits, it hits hard.

The bottom line is this: our culture encourages us to constantly be chasing after the next best thing. If we stay too long in one season, we appear to be left behind.

Graduation can't come soon enough.
I'm ready to get out of this town.
When I get the job - then I'll be content.
Once I shed ten more pounds, THEN I'll be happy.
When I'm in a relationship, I'll be happy.

We often hear the phrase "the grass is always greener" as it relates to contentment. Like hopping from dating to engagement to marriage, the moment you jump over to a new lawn, it's inevitable that you'll find another one that seems better. It's an endless game of leapfrog, which never truly satisfies.

But you *can* nurture your present place, starting with your mindset. This is why I believe that the quality of your grass has a lot more to do with the way you water and care for it, than the actual lawn itself.

Think about it: If we spend all of our days peering over our neighbor's fence, wondering how we got stuck over on this side, our grass is doomed to wither away. We get so distracted by lamenting what we don't have and neglect to care for what we *do* have. But if we pull out some weeds, give it a fresh cut, and lighten up the place with a few pink flamingos, we'll begin to nurture the grass, as well as our hearts.

We can live in bitterness, believing that God has neglected us. Or we plant pink flamingos of truth – that God is just, good, and righteous. That He cares for us, and He withholds no good thing. He gives good gifts. And He has perfect timing. He is sovereign, and He sees far more of the picture than we do.

The more rooted we are in the truths about God's character, the more joy we will find in our circumstances.

Despite what your feelings tell you, you aren't there alone. God has gone in before you, is following closely behind, and is holding your hand in the present wherever you are *(Deuteronomy 31:8)* because He cares about you.

So if you're ready to really start enjoying your life, come down from your tippy toes, and step away from your neighbor's fence. Step into your own reality, plant pink flamingos of truth, and find the joy that's waiting to be cultivated.

REMEMBER HIS SOVEREIGNTY

One of the reasons we can get stuck in discontentment is because our perspective is so inwardly focused. Our minds are fixated on how terrible our current situation is, and how much better a different situation would be. We focus so much on our personal injustice that we forget who God is. We forget that He is good, sovereign, loving, and just.

> "Yours, Lord, is the greatness and the power and the glory and the majesty and the splendor, for everything in heaven and earth is yours. Yours, Lord, is the kingdom; you are exalted as head over all." 1 Chronicles 29:11(NIV)

A few years ago, one of my closest friends was struggling with severe mental health issues. She was in so much pain, and I prayed night and day for her healing. But God wasn't answering my pleas. He did not take away her struggle or relieve her of the pain she was in. I didn't understand why He was holding out. I was angry, confused, bitter, and sad. *Why won't You do something, God?*

Early one morning, in the midst of this painful season, I found myself plopped down next to a stream of water in the middle of IU's campus. Eyes full of tears and heart full of frustration, I opened my Bible to the only place I knew where to turn for encouragement: The Psalms.

I landed in Psalm 23.

> "The Lord is my shepherd, I lack nothing. He makes me lie down in green pastures, he leads me beside quiet waters, he refreshes my soul. He guides me along the right paths for his name's sake. Even though I walk through the darkest valley, I will fear no evil, for you are with me; your rod and your staff, they comfort me. You prepare a table before me in the presence of my enemies. You anoint my head with oil; my cup overflows. Surely your goodness and love will follow me all the days of my life, and I will dwell in the house of the Lord forever." Psalm 23 (NIV)

This passage became my personal song. I memorized it, meditated on it, and repeated it to myself daily - sometimes hourly. I desperately clung to these words: *The Lord is my shepherd. Even though I walk through the valley of the shadow of death, I will fear no evil, for my God is with me.*

As I studied this scripture more, I noticed a pattern with the way it was written.

Verses 1-3 are focused on God's character: The Lord is my shepherd, I lack nothing. He makes me lie down in green pastures, he leads me beside quiet waters, he refreshes my soul. He guides me along the right paths for his name's sake.

Verse 4 is focused on the writer's predicament: Even though I walk through the darkest valley, I will fear no evil, for you are with me; your rod and your staff, they comfort me.

Verses 5-6 are focused on God's promises: You prepare a table before me in the presence of my enemies. You anoint my head with oil; my cup overflows. Surely your goodness and love will follow me all the days of my life, and I will dwell in the house of the Lord forever.

I've realized that the reason this passage was so comforting to me was because it focused very little on the writer's problem, and much more on the character and promises of God. As I meditated on this Psalm, I was encouraged by focusing more on God's character and promises, and less on my troubles.

So often we ruminate on our problems and how we wish our circumstances could be different. I think if we sandwiched this between remembering who God is, we would have so much more confidence and comfort in our circumstances.

What happened to my friend?
She suffered for a little while, but when God was ready, He began to heal her. Now she is using her story to empower other women, and share God's love and healing power with others. In the moment, God seemed absent and inactive. In retrospect, I now see that His timing was perfect, and even though He didn't heal her on *my* time; He *still* healed her. He remained true to His character and His promises, even when all I seemed to see was the turmoil.

Write about a time when you thought God was absent, or had abandoned your prayers?

Looking back, how did He make beauty out of that situation, using it for His glory?

What circumstances do you need to trust God with right now?

How can you *know* that He will turn it out for your good and His glory?

Using Psalm 23 as an example, formulate your own contentment sandwich here:

Who is God (what is His character like)?

What is my struggle or current circumstance?

What are some of God's promises?

We have a God of consistency. If He can make beauty out of Jesus' bloodshed, and heal my friend's psyche, He can surely make beauty out of whatever ashes you're holding on to. You are right where you're supposed to be *for your good and His glory,* because He is sovereign and He cares for you.

Prayer For The Day

Dear God,
Thank you for caring for me like a shepherd cares for his sheep.
Help me to trust in Your plan and remember that Your ways are
far greater, better, higher, and more beautiful than my own.
When I'm jealous of other's circumstances, help me remember
that You grow beauty from ashes if I choose to embrace the roots.
When my world feels out of control and there is nothing I can do,
help me to trust in Your sovereignty that keeps the planets and
stars in motion. I trust that if You can make good from an
innocent man's death on a cross, You can make good from my
situation too. Let these truths be my pink flamingos.
Amen.

YOU ARE IMPERFECT

"I'm so sorry." I said through tears, as I grabbed two plates and sat them on the counter. I wanted to have dinner ready the minute my husband walked through the door. After three months of marriage, I was supposed to have the routine down. Instead, we were eating an hour later than planned. To make matters worse, my husband helped me make the meal that I was trying to have prepared for him after his hard day at work.

"You don't have to apologize, Kelsee. I'm just glad to have this meal with you."

My husband did not expect me to have dinner ready at exactly 5:25. He didn't even expect me to make it all on my own and have it perfectly presented. *I put those harsh expectations on myself.*

As women, we have a tendency to impose lofty, demanding, and sometimes unrealistic expectations of perfection on ourselves. We must be the employee of the month – every month, and be the ultimate best friend – always ready to drop everything in order to be there for others. Anything less than a 4.0 in school is unacceptable; we must be able to fit into that one pair of jeans from senior year forever, and our 5K time is never allowed to slow down. We often do this with our roles as Christian women, too.

We expect to wake up every morning with a perfect hour of quiet time, studying the Bible, praying for every prayer request from small group, walking out the door singing worship songs, journaling pretty scriptures while we eat lunch, and never sinning - ever. And when that doesn't happen - which is often -

we believe this lie that we're terrible Christians, just like I believed I was a terrible wife the night we had a late dinner.

So from one recovering perfectionist to the next...I want to point out three lies we often believe about perfection.

Lie Number One: Perfection has a formula.

Perfection in this world is relative to each individual. To me, perfection often takes the form of happy relationships - if there is no conflict, no anger, no disappointments, everything will be perfect. But for my neighbor down the street, a perfect life might be measured by material possessions. We think we know exactly what perfection is, and if we adhere to a certain prescription, we will attain it. These prescriptions for perfection are often informed by our culture and media. But God's standard of perfection can't be formulated by good grades, a growing bank account, a healthy BMI, or peaceful relationships. In God's eyes, perfection is embodied by Jesus. God desires us to be just like Jesus. He created us in His image *(Genesis 1:27)* to pursue holiness. We are the ones who have decided to chase after worldly perfection instead.

Lie Number Two: If I achieve perfection, I will be satisfied.

If you've ever struggled with perfection yourself, you know that it takes up tons of energy and attention. Maybe you'll attain worldly perfection in one area of your life, but eventually, a different area is going to need that focus and attention. It's a vicious cycle of striving that is never complete...therefore, never satisfying.

Lie Number Three: I am capable of perfection.

Realistically, we'll never reach our worldly perfection. But even if we could...even if that was possible...we still wouldn't be perfect enough for God, because His standard is Jesus. Even our best worldly perfection falls flat to the standard that God has for us. Jesus is the only one truly capable of meeting God's standard of perfection.

I realize all this talk about imperfection might feel a little "Negative Nancy." Our world, and especially the American culture, idolizes perfection and trains us from a very young age to believe that perfection is what makes us worthy of love.

Although God desires perfection and holiness for us, He isn't surprised when we fail to meet His standard. He knows it is a high standard. He sees our imperfections but loves us through them. On *Day 10*, we'll be discussing in more detail how exactly God loves us through our imperfection and brokenness.

In the meantime, soak in this promise: We have a God of restoration, making all things pure and new; and that newness includes YOU *(Revelation 21:4-5)*.

REMEMBER CHRIST'S RIGHTEOUSNESS

The following verse says that God is transforming us into the image of Christ.

> "And we all, who with unveiled faces contemplate the Lord's glory, **are being transformed into his image** with ever-increasing glory, which comes from the Lord, who is the Spirit." 2 Corinthians 3:18 (NIV, Emphasis added)

Make a list describing Jesus. *I've started the list for you.*

Reliable (He fulfilled prophecies.)

Perfect

How does it make you feel to imagine being transformed in a way that reflects the image of Jesus?

Even though we won't be fully like Christ until we are in heaven, we are still meant to try our best, by the power of Holy Spirit, to be a mirror image of Christ for the world to see right here, right now *(2 Corinthians 5:20)*. There is grace for us, yet holiness is still our standard.

What are three ways you can reflect Jesus in your everyday life?

When the weight of perfection gets you down, and it seems like too much to bear, remember that Jesus is our only standard. Hold onto this glimpse of Jesus' character, and find hope by remembering that although you are imperfect now, there will be a day when you will be clothed in Christ's righteousness.

Prayer For The Day

Dear Lord,
I know I am following all the wrong standards of perfection. Jesus is the one true standard. Help me to break free from the enslavement of worldly perfectionism. Allow me to humble myself, remembering that Your son is the embodiment of perfection. Help me to look forward to the day that You complete the work of becoming like Jesus in me. I know this transformation is only possible because of Your grace and His sacrifice. Thank You. Give me a desire to strive for holiness here on Earth, and represent You well, with Jesus as my example.
Amen.

YOU ARE LOVED

"I love you."

It's amazing what kind of power is packed into these three little words. Love can make us do incredible things. Love can give a mother the supernatural power to save her baby under extreme circumstances. Love can enable us to selflessly put another person's needs and desires before our own – something that doesn't come naturally to most humans. Likewise, even the *search* for love can cause us to act in radical ways. We may change who we are depending on whose love we are trying to earn. We may do things we said we'd never do in order to feel that warm fuzzy feeling of love - I know that one all too well.

There have been times in my life when I would do anything in order to feel loved. This behavior led me into a relationship with a guy who did not treat me well. He was controlling, manipulative, and caused me to question my self-worth. But I believed the good times we had together were really good. I wanted to have more of those good times, so I began to change myself. I altered the language I used, the way I dressed and acted, and compromised certain beliefs that I had in order to feel loved by this boy. I deceived my parents and others around me in order to make everything seem okay - all for the sake of feeling loved.

Why do we go to such great lengths in order to be loved?

We were wired for love. God created us with a desire for relationship - to give love and receive love. Unfortunately, our recognition of what love is has been lost in translation. It's been skewed by romantic comedies, novels, and love songs on the radio. As a result, we're looking for a love that we can recognize in this world: approving parents, head over heels fiancé, and inseparable friends. We're looking for a love that we can tangibly feel - hand holding, belly laughing, flowers on our doorstep, letters in the mailbox, kisses goodnight, and surprise birthday parties. We're looking for a love that we can define and bottle up. But true love doesn't look like a diamond ring or daddy daughter dances. If it did, some people would never have a chance.

Jesus is clear when He teaches about love. He says it is sacrificial and unconditional. It is unwavering, and perfect love even has the power to drive out all fear *(1 Corinthians 13:4-8 and 1 John 4:18).*

My encouragement to you today is this: You may or may not be boyfriend loved, best friend loved, or dad loved...But you are, in fact, *Savior* loved.

Jesus said there is no greater love in this world than to lay down your life for another *(John 15:13).* He did that for *you*, so that you would know exactly how loved you are. He loves you when you aren't easy to love - in your sin. He loves you when He has every right and power to walk away.

As you may imagine, my relationship with that boy did not last, but Jesus was there, waiting to pick up the pieces of my wounded heart, and ready to rebuild them into something beautiful.

I'm not sure what kind of heartaches *you've* experienced, but I can tell you there is no greater comfort to the pain of this world than the arms of your loving Savior. He is a Loyal Friend and Soothing Counselor. He is the Prince of Peace and Deliverer of

Justice. His hands that filled the ocean and formed the mountain range are the same hands that will mend your hurting heart, and like anything else He touches, He'll make it beautiful, because He loves you.

REMEMBER GOD'S SACRIFICE

Let's take a look at how God's love compares to the world's definition of love.

> "Greater love has no one than this: to lay down one's life for one's friends."
> John 15:13 (NIV)

List some characteristics of love according to this world. I've started a few for you:

It's a trade: Your love for my love.

It is based on feelings and opinion.

What are some underline biblical characteristics of love? (See 1 Corinthians 13:4-8)

Sacrificial

Patient

What differences do you notice between the two?

The book of Hosea in the Bible tells the story of a man who God sent to marry a woman whom he knew would be unfaithful to him. Hosea obeyed God and married this woman named Gomer. As predicted, Gomer left her husband, but not just for any man...Gomer left her husband and became a prostitute! Just let that sink in for a moment.

But Hosea's commitment to his wife was unwavering. He purchased her back from prostitution - TWICE, until she finally realized his love for her and began to love him herself.

Hosea was an *active prophet*. This means that God sent him to live out this life so that it would be a powerful, eye opening message to Israel, and to us: Gomer, the adulterous wife represents us in the story, and Hosea, the faithful husband, represents *God*.

We are constantly wandering from one man-made version of love to another in hopes of finding "the one." We are rebellious, desperate, prideful, and selfish. We so often flee from God's perfect love, and into the arms of idols that we believe will serve us better. Yet like God picked up my broken pieces, and like Hosea carried his wife out of a brothel, God is always faithful - waiting to pick up your broken pieces.

The title of today's devotion is: *You Are Loved,* but it could easily have been named *You Are Broken*. I didn't call it that because I already called you imperfect, and you probably didn't buy this book for titles like that.

But the reality is that we'll never understand how deeply loved we are, if we don't first understand how broken we are. We are sinful - every single one of us. Our sin is offensive to God. It's repulsive! We are like an adulterous bride who became a prostitute.

But our Prince loves us so much that He would do anything to have a relationship with us. He doesn't stop loving us. He doesn't stop pursuing us. He doesn't give up on us. Instead, He walks right into the brothel – the depths of our sin - laying down the payment and purchasing us back.

What was the price? He died a gruesome, humiliating, and torturous death on a wooden cross as payment to deliver you from darkness, exchanging His life for yours.

Greater love is none than THIS. There's no greater love!

But His love for you did not stop at the cross. As if that wasn't a big enough statement of love...three days later, when all hope seemed lost, Jesus rose from the grave *(Luke 24)*. In doing so, Jesus proved that He was God. He did this so that more people would believe in Him. And He did this so that you could spend an eternity in heaven where there would be no more suffering, tears, cancer, death, heartache, divorces, murder, sickness, depression, or brokenness *(Revelation 21:4)*.

He loves you so much that He came back from the grave so that your life wouldn't have to end here.

This love is the fundamental characteristic of God that we've been studying over the last ten days, and the driving force behind every single piece of your identity. His love, and His love alone, is what gives you an identity.

Accepting that you are loved begins with accepting that you are broken and sinful. (1 John 1:8)
What are some sins, or wrongdoings, that you need forgiveness for?

Jesus paid the penalty for these sins out of His abundant love for you. What does it mean to you that a perfect God loves a sinful girl like you (and me) to the point of willingly dying a painful death?

Use the space below to thank God for His forgiveness and relentless love.

In the heartbreaks of this world, how might remembering God's love help you persevere?

When this world tries to tell you that you are not loved, remember that you *are* loved because of His son. Your brokenness and His sacrifice are proof of how deep and unending His love for you is. God's sacrifice, His son's death and resurrection, powerfully and permanently display that you are loved.

Prayer For The Day

Dear God,
Thank you for loving me. This can sometimes be the hardest truth to believe, but Your death on the cross convinces me over and over again. Help me to choose Your love over any other kind of love. Remind me that I don't need to take any drastic measures in order to be loveable because You've already proven me to be loved to the point of death. When I start to let lies about love creep into my mind, help me to remember Your truth. Help me to love others the way You've loved me, and help me to love You in return.
Your Daughter

CONCLUSION

MY PRAYER FOR YOU

Thank you for joining me for *10 Days of Remembering Who God Says You Are.* I hope that you were encouraged and challenged along the way.

The cry of my heart is that regardless of how long you've been a Christian, you now know more about the Lord, and more about how He see's you, than when you first opened this devotional. I hope that the power of remembrance has been revealed to you in a personal way, and that you now understand the link between who God is and who He says you are. I pray that God's character would be the reinforcement you need to truly believe in the identity He has given you:

His pursuit proves that you are chosen.
You are enough because of His grace.
Your victories are evidence of your potential.
Our inerrant creator, God, wonderfully designed you.
His power makes you strong.
You are an important part of God's mission.
You are on the winning team in the war of good
and evil.
Because He is sovereign, you can trust that you are cared for in all circumstances.
You are imperfect, but thanks to Jesus' sacrifice, you will be clothed in His righteousness someday.
God's sacrifice proves, in the most magnificent way, that you are loved.

Finally, I hope that this was just the beginning of your new habit of actively and intentionally remembering God. I hope that when the voices of the enemy start to creep in, and our competitive culture becomes overbearing, you would find this devotional tucked away on your bookshelf and flip through the stories that you've documented - boosting your memory again and again until you are united with Christ, and like His disciples, don't need a reminder anymore. You can boast – not in your own man-made worthiness, but in Christ's worthiness, which shines upon you. Because of *His* infinite worth, you are made worthy.

With Love & Freedom,
Kelsee

ACKNOWLEDGEMENTS

The Lord has allowed me to share this life with some of the most remarkable people; many of you helped bring the words of this book to life and paper.

Quinn - Thank you for embracing my dreams as your own, and for nudging me outside of my comfort zone – always with gentleness and confidence. I love you.

My sweet mentors, Cheri and Amy - your friendships mean the world to me. Thank you for teaching, sharpening, encouraging, and above all else, inspiring me. Your generosity, and your devotion to heart-change are both contagious.

Vicki Stone of Proofing for Pros, and the rest of the Grit 'n' Grace Girls Ministry Team - I'm so glad to call you my sisters.

Momma - I spent endless hours of my childhood with books in my lap (we had the library late fees as proof). You gave me one the greatest gifts: a love for words. Thank you.

Mallory - you are my soul sister. You've showed me the true power of authenticity in friendship, and that sisterhood is always a cause worth fighting for.

Caitlin, Sinikka, Alex G., Rachel - you are image bearers of God's creative heart. Thank you for sharing your gifts with me.

NEXT STEPS

Would you like to learn more about your identity in Christ or how to make *remembrance* a habit in your life?

Here are some ideas for your next steps:

Find a church
Sunday morning worship is a great way to learn about God, worship Him, and remember Him through biblical teaching.

Join a small group
We were made for community, so it's natural that we learn about God from one another.

Find a mentor
Find an older woman who is strong in her faith and displays characteristics you'd like to attain. Tell her what you admire in her, and ask if she'd be willing to meet with you regularly.

Get in the Word
Buy a Bible or open the one you already have! Reading God's word is the best way to know Him and remember what He has done.

Start a prayer journal
Writing down prayer requests and praises is a great way to remember God's faithfulness. It's like a handwritten scrapbook that you can look back and see God's character and promises played out in your life!

Share this message
If the last ten days impacted you positively at all, share it with another lady in your life. Lead a younger gal by going through this devotional with her. Multiply God's goodness by sharing it with others.

FREE GIFT FOR YOU

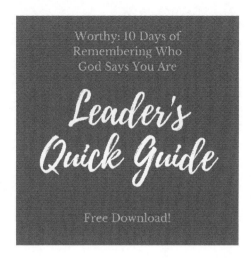

Worthy can be easily formatted to fit within the structure of a small group. If you would like to lead a number of women in a *Worthy* study, this resource is for you!

Visit www.kelseekeitel.com/resources/worthydev otional/ to download your free *Leader's Quick Guide,* for Kelsee's guidance through a ten-week small group study of identity and remembrance.

ABOUT THE AUTHOR

Photo by Caitlin Tyner

Kelsee Keitel resides in Indianapolis, IN with her husband, Quinn, where she is pursuing a graduate degree in counseling. An Evansville, IN, native, and a graduate of Indiana University, she is a Hoosier through and through.

When she isn't studying, Kelsee enjoys writing and speaking through her ministry *Detangled & Free*, guest writing for other blogs, and mentoring young women through *Cru*.

Kelsee is most often found snuggled up under a fuzzy blanket with hot tea and a book in hand, mid-phone call with her mom, testing out new recipes, or rock climbing with Quinn. Those who know her best would describe Kelsee as sweet and quirky, probably due to her love of donuts and affection for earthworms.

Connect with Kelsee on a daily basis through social media:

Blog: www.kelseekeitel.com

Facebook: www.facebook.com/kelseedetangled

Instagram: @detangledandfree @kelseerk

ABOUT DETANGLED & FREE

Detangled & Free empowers women to choose sisterhood over competition – exchanging jealousy, comparison, and shame for the freedom found in Christ. Like a tangled necklace, jealousy and comparison leave women feeling trapped. Detangled & Free explores how women can find freedom from the sin that entangles them by following Jesus. (Hebrews 12:1-3)

Worthy was Kelsee's response to a number of comments and conversations had through Detangled & Free. She realized that a major reason why women feel jealous is because they aren't rooted in their Christ-given identity.

If you were inspired by *Worthy* and would like to tackle the tricky struggle of comparison and jealousy in your life, Detangled & Free is for you.

Detangled & Free exists to be a safe place for you to bring darkness into light and take practical steps toward freedom. This is only done through the power and grace of God, with the gospel message at the center of every blog post and resource.

For more information about Detangled & Free, visit kelseekeitel.com.

Kelsee loves speaking to women at universities, high schools, and churches. To inquire about having Kelsee speak at your event, visit www.kelseekeitel.com/contact/

Made in the USA
Columbia, SC
28 December 2017